Christmas Nativity Innsbruck

Cristina Berna and Eric Thomsen

2024

Christmas Nativity

Innsbruck

Cristina Berna and Eric Thomsen

Copyright ©2018, 2021, 2024 **Cristina Berna and Eric Thomsen**

All rights reserved. Without limiting the rights under copyright reserved above, no part of this publication may be reproduced, stored in or introduced into a retrieval system, or transmitted, in any form, or by any means (electronic, mechanical, photocopying, recording or otherwise) without the prior written permission of both the copyright owner and the above publisher of this book.

ISBN 978-0-5771-3340-0

This title is available in color in the United States under ISBN 978-1-956-215-830 and in the European Union under ISBN 978-3-757862-55-8

About the authors

Cristina Berna loves photographing and writing. She also creates designs and advice on fashion and styling.

Eric Thomsen has published in science, economics and law, created exhibitions and arranged concerts.

Also by the authors:

World of Cakes

Luxembourg – a piece of cake

Florida Cakes

Catalan Pastis – Catalonian Cakes

Andalucian Delight

World of Art

Hokusai – 36 Views of Mt Fuji
and other titles

Outpets

Deer in Dyrehaven – Outpets in Denmark

Florida Outpets

Birds of Play

Vehicles

Copenhagen vehicles – and a trip to Sweden

Construction vehicles picture book

Trains
and other titles

Missy's Clan

Missy's Clan – The Beginning

Missy's Clan – Christmas

Missy's Clan – Education

Missy's Clan – Kittens

Missy's Clan – Deer Friends

Missy's Clan – Outpets

Missy's Clan – Outpet Birds
and other titles

Christmas

Christmas Nativities Barcelona

Christmas Nativities Malaga

Christmas Nativities Sevilla

Christmas Nativities Madrid

Christmas Nativities Luxembourg Trier

Christmas Nativity United States

Christmas Market Innsbruck
and other titles

Contact the authors

missysclan@gmail.com

Published by www.missysclan.net

Cover picture: The Holy Family, nativity at Holzschnitsereien Strobl, Innsbruck, Austria

Inside: Jaufenthaler Krippe, Christmas Market on the market square, Innsbruck, Austria

Content

Introduction	8
Short history	10
Austria	17
Innsbruck	19
Jaufenthaler Krippe	26
Christmas Market at the market square	31
Christmas Market in the Old Town	35
Shop Windows	46
Other Ornaments	61

Introduction

One of the wonderful traditions of Christmas is the Nativity. But you don't have to be Christian or a regular church-goer to love these wonderful displays. The creativity and artistry speak to all children and to the child in us all.

Nativity is a scene from the stories of the birth of Jesus. They are in the Gospels of Matthew and Luke. With inspiration in these stories you use either figurines or live people to create the scene and convey the story.

These scenes excite especially the children. Their happy smiles and their joy is so wonderfully rewarding. But adults as well enjoy both creating and looking at the nativity scenes.

This has developed into a huge handicraft industry in countries like Spain and Italy. Artists and craftsmen work all year round to create their next exhibits, which are sold especially at Christmas markets.

Families collect figurines and accessories from the markets and create their own displays at home. Churches, beginning with the Vatican, and cities and other institutions create their own annual exhibits that are venerated and celebrated.

This little book shows you some of the nativity scenes we have seen and some of the figurines and accessories that you can find in the various Christmas markets and shops in Innsbruck, Austria.

Nativity is today a Catholic tradition, separated in many countries from official society as Christianity does no longer have the same central function, although the European values and norms are deeply steeped in Christianity.

In Northern European countries the birth of Jesus is no longer the central theme of the Christmas displays.

We show you also some alternative displays, usually with animals, that are used instead to make the children, and adults, happy. Mostly they are in shopping windows and displace for a while the display of some of the commercial goods that is the daily function of the windows.

Cristina and Eric

Short history

Saint Francis of Assisi is often credited with being the first to create a live nativity scene, in 1223. He did it to promote the worship of Christ. He had come back from The Holy Land, where he had been shown the traditional birthplace of Jesus. The scene was so popular that it inspired communities throughout Catholic countries to stage similar pantomimes.

The nativity tradition thus started in the late Middle Ages in Italy. Italy is still one of the countries with the strongest nativity traditions, although of course "Italy" back then was not quite the same as it was under the Roman Empire or what it is now.

The Middle Ages is a long historic period in Europe starting abt 500 AD with the fall of the Western Roman Empire and lasting to abt 1500 AD when the Renaissance and the Age of Discovery took over.

Bartolomé Esteban Murillo: (1617-1682): Saint Francis Embracing Christ on the Cross (1668), Museo de Bellas Artes de Seville, Spain. https://commons.wikimedia.org/wiki/File:Stfrancisembrace1668.jpg

Catholic Christianity ruled most of Western Europe in those days – and religion very much organized everybody's lives back then.

The Welcoming of Christ the Child at the beginning of the four Sundays of Advent that ends with Christmas Day, which is the 25 December is one of the most important celebrations in the year.

Catholicism came to dominate Western Europe as The Roman Empire disintegrated. Catholicism is the teaching of the Bishop of Rome – there were five bishops in the early Christian World, and the Bishop in Rome became the Pope.

The Roman Empire was divided in two by Diocleatian in 284 AD. He believed the empire was too large to rule for one man and created the tetrarchy – a four man rule – with two rulers in the west (Maximian and Constantius the Pale) and two in the east (himself and Galerius).

Convinced of his own success he abdicated and soon the tetrarchy collapsed.

Monument to the first living nativity scene in Greccio north of Rome, staged by Saint Francis of Assisi in 1223
.https://commons.wikimedia.org/wiki/File:Greccio_10-07_to_22_776.jpg

Constantine eventually restored order and became emperor in 305 AD and was the first Roman emperor who converted to Christianity.

In Europe the border between the Western and Eastern Roman empires was made up by the Sava river and parts of the *Drini* river that flows into the Sava river, today part of the border between Bosnia and Herzegovina and Serbia.

Emperor Constantine who ruled until 337 AD is known as Constantine I or Constantine the Great. He re-founded Byzantium as "New Rome" until it became Constantinople.

Constantine promoted Christendom heavily and is often called the first Christian emperor. He called the first council of Nicaea in 325 AD which produced the Nicene Creed. The Nicene Creed affirms the doctrine of the holiness of the Son together with that of the Farther, the co-holiness of Jesus together with God.

The Eastern Roman empire was created 11 May 330 AD, and continued until 1453 AD, when it fell to the Ottoman Turks. The Byzantine empire was the most powerful economic, cultural and military power in Europe for the most of the thousand years it survived the fall and disintegration of the Western Roman empire.

Western Europe forgot almost all about the Eastern Roman empire even though Byzantine had lands in Italy for a long time and all the accumulated wisdom and knowledge as Western Europe sank into barbary and ignorance.

The first university in Western Europe was founded in Bologna, Italy in 1088, more than 500 years after the collapse of the Western Roman empire to the invading Frank and Germanic tribes. Most people had no inkling about what was going on in Byzantine or what treasures of knowledge and wisdom was kept alive there, like in the field of law.

The great emperor Charlemagne, 2 April 742 AD – 28 January 814 AD, is an important beacon in Western European history and culture. He unified most of Western and Central Europe through almost continuous military campaigning during his reign, only to create the chaos that has plagued Western Europe since his death, by dividing his empire between his three sons, roughly into France, Germany and Italy.

It can not be emphasized enough just how important the Catholic Church was for the reorganization of Western Europe after the collapse of the Western Roman Empire.

The church provided order and security after the chaos. It took care of the spiritual needs of the people and became a powerful political force, which it can be argued was later to become a burden.

However, by its powerful political influence it had influence over the powerful secular rulers, whom it could excommunicate and effectively make outcasts and then potential victims of other rulers that could take their lands.

The monks and nuns devoted their lives to prayers and good deeds and thereby founded the traditional European norms and values.

Austria

We will continue our story of the Nativity in Austria, after having published the first book about Nativities in Spain.

Austria is today a smaller country with 8.7 mio inhabitants compared to the 47 mio in Spain.

The mighty rock *Kufstein* on the border between German and Austria, on the way to Innsbruck. ©Berna 2018

But Austria was once part of the Holy Roman Empire, ruled by the Habsburgs.

The Habsburgs have a strong connection to Spain and that is a good reason to continue our story in Austria.

We will begin by visiting Innsbruck, a thriving city in the Western part of Austria, called Tyrol.

The access is mainly via the German motorway that connects Munchen in Bavaria with Salzburg, Austria, on the way to Vienna.

The Austria Empire was first dismembered by Bismarck, when he assembled Germany and again after World War I.

The empire lost Czechoslovakia, Hungary and Slovenia which became independent countries and the Italian Tyrol, which became part of Italy.

When it was the Holy Roman Empire and in 1648 included Germany, the Northern part was Protestant – Calvinist and Lutheran - and the rest mainly Catholic. When in 1870 it was Austria-Hungary 90 per cent in Austria and 60 per cent in Hungary were Catholic.

Innsbruck

The town of Innsbruck has its name because it was here there was a bridge – *bruck* – over the river *Inn*. Inn springs near St Moritz and confluence with the Danube at Passau on the border to Bavaria in Southern Germany.

The bridge *Innsbrucke* is just past the market square with the main Christmas market, where we found some of the first Nativity figurines.

Dec 2018 River Inn from *Innbrucke,* Innsbruck ©Berna 2018

Innsbruck was an important trading post on the *Brenner pass* route to Italy, some 30 km to the South, the easiest crossing of the Alps. It was part of the *via Imperi* under special protection of the king and the revenues led the city to flourish.

Innsbruck has been populated since the early Stone Age, which lasted 3.4 million years and ended with the metal ages. Copper smelting started in nearby Serbia 7.000 BC.

Innsbruck was established as a market place in 1133 when the Counts of Andechs bought a field on the left bank of the Inn, today called St. Nikolaus.

The Counts of Andechs were German princes with possessions in Istria and on the Dalmatian seacoast.

In 1180 they swopped land with the Priory of Wilten to make a market on the Southern bank.

The market and the trading rights were mentioned in a document in 1187 and between this year and 1205 the market eventually got city rights.
Innsbruck became a privileged town, not just a field with trading rights.

In 1248 Innsbruck passed to the Counts of Tyrol, which is an estate in the Habsburg lands.

Habsburg Holy Roman Emperor Maximillian I - 22 March 1459 – 12 January 1519, resided here. He was Holy Roman Emperor from 1508 to his death.

This is the European period of *Renaissance*, from French – rebirth – following the Middle Ages.

Maximillian I was not as usual crowned by the Pope in Rome, but instead in Trent on the other side of Brenner pass, part of Habsburg lands, because the journey to Rome was too risky.

Dec 2018 Herzog-Siegmund-Ufer, Innsbruck ©Berna 2018

He expanded the influence of the Habsburgs, who by the way came from Switzerland, where there is still a castle – *burg* – by that name.

Maximillian I gained Burgundy and the Netherlands though marriage. He married his son Philippe the Handsome to Joanna of Castille in 1498 and established the Habsburgs on the Spanish throne. His son wanted to be king of Castille and was killed by his father in law, Ferdinand II of Aragon, to avert a civil war.

However, Maximillian I lost the Austrian territories of what is today Switzerland, to the Swiss Confederacy in the Battle of Dornach 22 July 1499 and by a peace treaty signed in Basel 22 September 1499 the Swiss Confederacy obtained independence from the Holy Roman Empire.

Maximillian I lived in Innsbruck which was the capital. Ferdinand I moved to Vienna in 1556, but before Prague had been capital of the Holy Roman Empire since the Luxembourg emperors, see the book *Luxembourg – A Piece of Cake*.

Dec 2018 Innsbruck Altstadt ©Berna 2018

Ferdinand I was the younger son of Philippe the Handsome and Joanna of Castille and born in Alcala de Henares.

Joanna was daughter of the Catholic kings, Ferdinand and Isabella, who reconquered Granada, the last piece of Spain that was conquered by the Muslims after 711 AD.

The elder brother was Charles V, who fought incessant wars in Germany and paid enormous bribes to the treasonous electors to become Holy Roman Emperor, and he never succeeded, but instead bankrupted the Spanish Empire with all the possessions in Latin America. He abdicated in 1556 and Ferdinand I took the title "Emperor Elect" from 1558. The Spanish Empire, the two Sicilies, the Netherlands and France Comte went to Philip, Charles' son.

Ferdinand I was initially Charles V's representative in Austria and Slovenia, the Habsburg hereditary lands, as Archduke of Austria 1521 – 1563

He ruled as king of Hungary and Bohemia, from 1526 – 1564, elected king conditioned on upholding the Bohemian privileges and in return they pledged to help him fight the Ottoman invasion of Hungary.

Ferdinand was challenged to the Hungarian throne by John Zápolya, a voivode from Transylvania, elected by a diet of lesser nobility in 1526. Ferdinand was short of money and soldiers, but borrowed from the Fugger bankers and got help from his brother Charles. He beat John Zápolya in the Battle of Tarcal September 1527 and again in the Battle of Szina March 1528.

John Zápolya fled to Turkey and appealed to sultan Suleyman the Magnificent and pledged Hungary as a vasal state.

Suleyman besieged Vienna but was famously beaten in 1529 - this is where the story of the *Croissant* comes from – and again in 1532 at Guns. Ferdinand I made peace with the Ottomans and Hungary was split into the Habsburg part and a vasal state of Turkey under John Zápolya.

Although he did not succeed in driving the Muslims from Hungary, Ferdinand was a much better ruler than his brother and more tolerant of various Christian practices.

Jaufenthaler Krippe

Dec 2018 Jaufenthaler Krippe, Innsbruck Markt ©Berna 2018

There are many children and parents waiting in the cold.

The children have to wait until 16:00 before Mary appears with the infant Jesus.

It is all automatic. When the time comes, the doors open to the stable and the Holy Family will appear. Until then you only have the donkey and the ox lying to the left of the door.

The children are waiting for *the Jauffenthaler Krippe* – the Jauffenthaler Nativity Scene – to start.

Dec 2018 Jaufenthaler Krippe, Innsbruck Markt ©Berna 2018

The mobile Jaufenthaler nativity scene (Jaufenthaler Krippe) can be admired at Advent on the Christmas market on the Innsbruck market square.

The nativity scene is a gift from the artist Friedrich Jaufenthaler, who died in 2004, to all children in Innsbruck and vividly depicts the birth of Jesus.

Jaufenthaler invested several thousand hours in the 7 x 3 meter crib, which impresses with its 28 engine-powered figurines.

Dec 2018 Jaufenthaler Krippe, Innsbruck Markt ©Berna 2018

Especially worth seeing are the "moving waterfall, the rise of the high altar or the appearance of the angel.

The opening ceremony always takes place on the 1st Advent Sunday, and after that the nativity scene can be admired every day between 16:00 and 19:00. The animation takes place every hour on the hour.

The Jaufenthaler nativity is on view until the 6th of January, when the Three Holy Kings arrive.

Dec 2018 Jaufenthaler Krippe, Innsbruck Markt ©Berna 2018

Now the time is just past 16:00 and the electric stable door has opened.

You see the infant Jesus in his little crib, with an angel in pink, with golden wings, hovering by his head.

To the right is the Holy Virgin Mary and to the left stands Josef with his staff.

In addition to the organized crib tinkerers, however, there are also the nativity outsiders who can always be found in Tyrol. Friedrich Jaufenthaler was such an outsider.

A crib for the home, as decoration in the best room in the house was much too small for him.

Friedrich Jaufenthaler built Jauffenthaler Krippe with quite sophisticated technology doe the time, the 1980s.

It has a total of 15 motors from washing machines, mixers, windshield wipers etc. used to create the movement on Krippenberg. So his moon slowly rises from an old radio with the help of the wave switch ...

There is even a film, where the artist explains how his Nativity works.

Christmas Market at the market square

Dec 2018 Kristkindl Markt, Innsbruck Marktplatz ©Berna 2018

The usual place to hunt for Nativity figurines is the annual Christmas market in Catholic countries. They have been going on from in Southern Herman speaking countries since the late Middle Ages. The Christmas market in Munich is mentioned first in 1310, but there was a December market in Vienna already in 1298.

Innsbruck was a market since 1133 so maybe they had religious objects for sale even then.

This stall in the Christmas market on the market square in Innsbruck sells hand made nativity scenes and other figurines with the proceeds benefitting children with cancer.

Dec 2018 Kristkindl Markt, Innsbruck Marktplatz ©Berna 2018

There is probably no greater horror for parents than their child is diagnosed with cancer. This heartbreaking fate demands extra strength and care. In most countries it is also a very expensive condition to treat and there is a great need for charities that can help in such a situation. Christmas is a good time to donate.

Dec 2018 Kristkindl Markt, Innsbruck Marktplatz ©Berna 2018

The nativity figurines in the charity stall are naïve and smiling, rounded figures and rounded faces.

They convey happiness and gratitude to the onlooker, an eternal "thank you!" for the purchase and the donation.

This will kindle the heart of the patron to remember why he bought precisely this nativity scene and his good wishes will forever flow to the children. Giving is the celebrated spirit of Christmas. It is the season where everybody remembers they are members of a greater society and we all have a responsibility for the World.

Dec 2018 Innbrücke and Dom St Jakob – St Jacob Cathedral in the background, Innsbruck ©Berna 2018

Christmas Market in the Old Town

Close by the Christmas market in the Altstadt – the Old City - is the *Hofkirche*- the Court Church.

Dec 2018 *Hofkirche* – Court Church - Innsbruck ©Berna 2018

The Hofkirche is a church in Gothic style in the Altstadt section of Innsbruck, Austria, Universitätsstraße 2. The church was built in 1553 by Emperor Ferdinand I as a memorial to his grandfather Emperor Maximilian I, whose cenotaph within boasts a remarkable collection of German Renaissance sculpture.

As the Hofkirche was built in the Renaissance period, the Gothic style was a deliberate choice from an earlier period.

Maximillian's will stipulated he be buried in Wiener Neustadt, but it was not practicable to build a great mausoleum there.

Maximilian's simple tomb remained in Wiener Neustadt and the Hofkirche serves as a cenotaph.

Dec 2018 Stall at Christkindl Markt Innsbruck ©Berna 2018

Dec 2018 Christkindl Markt Innsbruck detail ©Berna 2018

Here you see typical examples of the Tyrolian wood carving styles.

There is a Nativity in a hollowed out piece of wood to the right.

You have Mary, sitting with the infant Jesus and the donkey lying down.

To the left you have Josef, standing and with a sheep behind him. On top the guiding star showing the way for the Holy Three Kings.

The same design is repeated, in a smaller version.

Further left you have slices of wood trunk with a very sweet rendition of the Holy Family.

Finally, far left, you have a piece if a thick branch decorated to look like a burning candle, with several versions of the Holy Family, silhouetted or painted relief.

Dec 2018 Christkindl Markt Innsbruck detail ©Berna 2018

Here you see variations of sweet angels holding various objects – a rocking horse – surely a Christmas present – playing a flute, holding a sheet of paper probably sheet music, holding a small doll or child, praying or playing the fiddle.

Dec 2018 Nativity scene in a gateway, Innsbruck ©Berna 2018

Above is a large nativity on the wall in a gate way, carved in flat wood. Not for sale, of course. It is a decoration of the building. Religious art is very prominent in Innsbruck because it was a highly Catholic part of Europe due to the Habsburgs.

Dec 2018 Christkindl Markt Innsbruck Altstadt ©Berna 2018

There are maybe 20 of the 70 stalls that display wood carved Nativity figurines and other Christmas decorations.

The wood handicrafts are very important.

It makes one compare with the Spanish Christmas markets, especially Malaga and Sevilla see *Christmas Nativities Spain*.

Some are more simple and some are exquisite works of art.

Dec 2018 Christkindl Markt Innsbruck Alysyadt ©Berna 2018

The stall manned by this girl was eye catching. There were different styles, but very detailed and elegant.

It is a cold job to man these stalls here in the Winter and the art work has been produced the rest of the year, so the life of the artist and the stall workers is a cycle just like farming and can span a whole life time.

This is the torch of tradition carried by generations for centuries.

Dec 2018 Christkindl Markt Innsbruck, detail ©Berna 2018

This wonderful stables have Mary kneeling by the manger with the infant Jesus. The Three Holy Kings are standing on either side of her.

There is the donkey and a sheep, and Josef or a shepherd to the left with a cow. There is an angel with a scroll to the right.

Dec 2018 Christkindl Markt Innsbruck Altstadt ©Berna 2018

Up on the shelf behind is a sweet Nativity and to the right a Nativity in white wood looking like ebony, and a couple of simple churches – but without the typical bulbed spires as are common in Tyrol. To the left a doll house like Nativity in two storeys.

Dec 2018 Nativity scene Innsbruck shop window ©Berna 2018

Here is from another stall one more of the complete Nativity scenes with a typical Tyrolian farm house instead of the Bethlehem stables. We have The Holy Family with the Three Holy Kings to the right. A local brown goat is nursing its kid.

To the left are locals, farmers or townspeople, an unusual variation, see *Christmas Nativities Spain*. An angel is watching from the gables.

Dec 2018 Stall at the Christmas market, Innsbruck Altstadt ©Berna 2018

Another of the many stalls with a rich variety of hand crafted Christmas Nativity figurines and ornaments

Dec 2018 Christmas market in Innsbruck Altstadt ©Berna 2018

Shop Windows

Apart from the Christmas markets there are some wonderful shop windows with Nativity figurines in Innsbruck.

Dec 2018   Nativity figurines in shop window in Innsbruck
©Berna 2018

Here are a number of complete Nativity scenes cast in the typical Tyrolian farm house.

Dec 2018 Nativity figurines in shop window in Innsbruck, detail
©Berna 2018

Here are many exquisite figurines, many of locals going about their natural business on the farm.

There are shepherds carrying lambs, one in a sling another over the shoulders.

There is a Holy Family in local old fashion dress, Josef with knickers, Mary in long petticoats. Other Holy Families are in dress looking more like what we imagine could be from Bethlehem at the time of Jesus's birth.

Dec 2018 Nativity scene, Innsbruck shop window ©Berna 2018

Here is a beautiful complete Nativity scene with a wintry Tyrolian farmhouse, with snow and icicles.

You see Mary and Josef in local old Tyrolian farm costume, with the infant Jesus in a rocking cradle.

There is a shepherd sitting with his hat to his chest and a wooden bucket in his other hand.

One of the Holy Three Kings is a boy is carrying the guiding star on a staff. Two other boy kings approach from the right after him.

On the loft are two children amusing themselves looking at the scene.

Dec 2018 Nativity scene, detail, Innsbruck shop window
©Berna 2018

To the left a bearded shepherd is approaching. The whole scene is beautiful and local Tyrolian probably 18th century.

Dec 2018 Nativity figurines and scenes, Innsbruck shop window
©Berna 2018

There are more shop windows with very good hand carved Nativity figurines.

There is a whole shop full of figurines of different types and sizes, and you will be sure to find something that you will like.

But they are one of a kind, not the many over the same theme as in the market stalls.

This is the sales window of an artist hand carver. There is the craftsman and there is the artist, which rises to the level above.

Dec 2018 Nativity scene, detail, Innsbruck shop window ©Berna 2018

Here is one set of Nativity figurines from the shop window display above.

The Holy Family is surrounded by the Three Holy Kings.

Unusual is that Josef is sitting by the infant Jesus and Mary is standing behind him. Maybe he is calling to her for something.

There is a little jug on a table, with a table cloth on it. It looks more like a painting, see on Murillo figurines in *Christmas Nativities Spain*.

Dec 2018 Nativity figurines, Jesus carrying the cross, detail, Innsbruck shop ©Berna 2018

This set of accessory figurines show Jesus carrying the cross and a Roman soldier. A female figurine is intervening with the soldier.

Two other figurines are standing about, taking part in the scene.

Dec 2018 Nativity figurines, detail, Innsbruck shop ©Berna 2018Female figurine carrying a basket, a man has fallen on his back, a bearded man looking to help, and a man carrying a jug.

Dec 2018 Nativity figurines, detail, Innsbruck shop ©Berna 2018

A black man – Balthazar? – and a blond female imploring. A man in pain – Jesus? – and a man holding him.

Dec 2018 The Last Supper, shop window, Innsbruck Altstadt
©Berna 2018

More incredible displays from the shop window.

A scene that looks like the Last Supper 1 Cor. 1:1-2, with people gathered around a table with a nice white cloth on it.

The place looks like a ruin, but that may be the architectural cut away to allow you to see, what is going on.

The Last Supper took place on Mount Zion just outside the walls of the Old City of Jerusalem in what is traditionally known as the Upper Room. It has been identified as a disused quarry.

Dec 2018 Detail from shop window, The Last Supper, Innsbruck Altstadt ©Berna 2018

Here is a detail of the supper scene. There are 13 figurines and one looks like a Jesus.

One is walking away from the group. This is Judas Iscariot who sneaked away to denounce Jesus to Caiaphus and the Head Priest.

The most famous is the mural by Leonardo da Vinci, in the Convent of Santa Maria delle Grazie in Milan, Italy, from the late 1490s. It represents the scene as told in the Gospel of St John 13:21. The scene has been a favorite of masters for centuries.

Dec 2018 Shop with Nativity figurines, Innsbruck Altstadt
©Berna 2018

In this detail there are two variations of the Holy Family as figurines as well as a carving in a flat piece of wood, a relief.

To the left Mary has the infant Jesus on her lap and a sheep is adoring him. Josef is a serene full bearded man.

In the center the Holy Family, coming together.

To the left a relief carved from flat wood.

Dec 2018 Wood relief Nativity, Innsbruck Altstadt ©Berna 2018

Here is another nativity carved in haut relief from a flat piece of wood. The faces are slightly grotesque.

Swarovski

The world famous Swarovski crystal glass business in Wattens near Innsbruck is a family owned business started in 1895. It employs some 25.000 people world wide and their products are represented in more than 3.000 shops.

Swarovski has sponsored the Christmas tree in the Innsbruck Christmas Market. It has also produced crystal Nativity sets. The pieces shown are from about 1991 – 1993. They are quite rare.

Swarowski Crystal Nativity set.

Tiroler Volkskunstmuseum in Innsbruck has an incredible collection of Nativity figurines, some exhibited in large Nativity scenes at the museum. Religious art has become one of the core areas of its focus.

Nativity scene at Tiroler Volkskunstmuseum in Innsbruck

Other Ornaments

Dec 2018 Stall at Christmas market, Innsbruck Altstadt ©Berna 2018

Dec 2018 Shop with Christmas décor in the Christmas market in the Old City, Innsbruck   ©Berna 2018

There are many other Christmas ornaments than just Nativity scenes and figurines.

There are all kinds of variations of ornaments for your Christmas tree, which in most families is more important than even the Nativity scene.

There are Christmas mugs for your hot mulled wine or warm tea, or just as a souvenir from Innsbruck Christmas market.

There is even a nice knitted warm hat or gloces.

Dec 2018 Shop with Christmas mugs, Innsbruck ©Berna 2018

On the way out an unusual display – looking like a horse, a deer, a St Bernard dog and a hawk.

Dec 2018 Christmas market, Innsbruck Altstadt ©Berna 2018

2018 Large size mesh animal sculptures, Innsbruck ©Berna Dec 2018

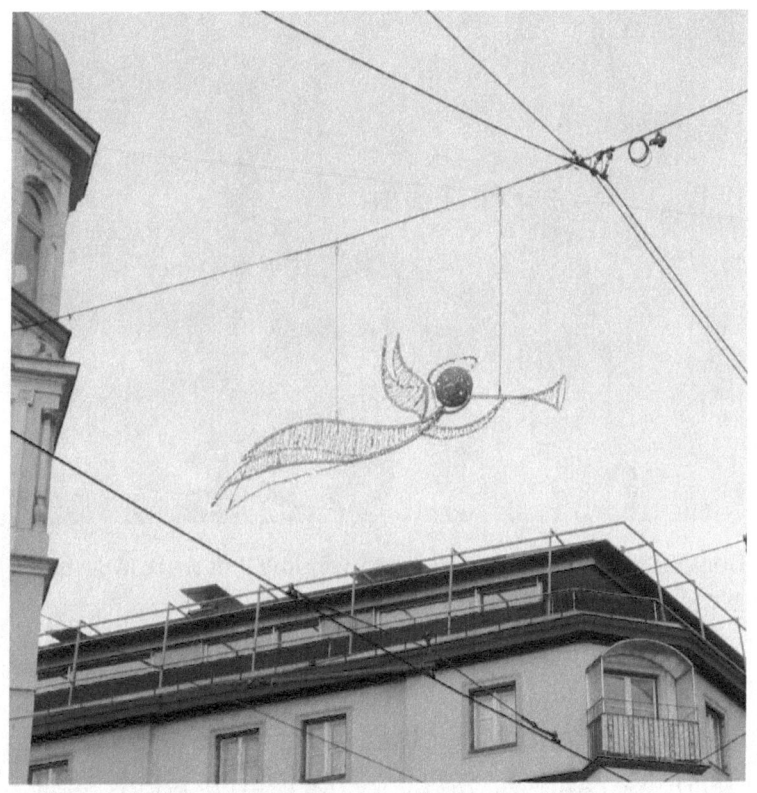

Dec 2018 Innsbruck Christmas angel in the sky ©Berna 2018

Above the streets there were stylized illuminations, here an angel blowing a trumpet.

All over Austria there are these illuminated Christmas decorations in many varieties, which supplements street illumination with a seasonal great experience.

Dec 2018 *Konditorei* - cake shop - window Innsbruck ©Berna 2018

The shop windows of other shops were also decorated and showed very decorative goods.

Here a cake shop - *Konditorei* – with beautifully packed chocolates.

Chocolates are a typical seasonal gift and they make the most wonderful chocolates in Innsbruck.

The highly artistic packaging contribute to the experience of the gift, thrilling the receiver both a reception and the later enjoyment.

Dec 2018   Cafeteria window Innsbruck ©Berna 2018

Here a cafeteria with colorful illuminated stars hanging around in a very decorative arrangement.

The expandable paper or carton Christmas star in which you can fit a light bulb is a popular Christmas ornament that you can buy also in the Christmas market. It is the guiding start that led the Holy Three Kings to the stall in Bethlehem with the infant Jesus in the Nativity Scene.

A white Nativity scene is displayed in front.

Dec 2013 A large wooden public nativity in a park a little away from the Old Town. ©Berna 2018

Christmas Nativity Hallstatt

ISBN 978-1-3549-3424-1

Cristina Berna and Eric Thomsen

2024

Christmas Market Malaga

ISBN 978-5-1068-3525-1

Cristina Berna and Eric Thomsen

2024

www.ingramcontent.com/pod-product-compliance
Lightning Source LLC
Chambersburg PA
CBHW020754230426
43665CB00009B/590